Vocals
Grade 1

Performance pieces, technical exercises and in-depth guidance for Rockschool examinations

To access audio visit:
www.rslawards.com/downloads

IC9LKI55RE

ISBN 978-1-78936-293-0

For all works contained herein:
Unauthorized copying, arranging, adapting, recording, internet posting, public performance,
or other distribution of the music in this publication is an infringement of copyright.
Infringers are liable under the law.

Visit Hal Leonard Online at
www.halleonard.com

World headquarters, contact:	In Europe, contact:	In Australia, contact:
Hal Leonard	**Hal Leonard Europe Limited**	**Hal Leonard Australia Pty. Ltd.**
7777 West Bluemound Road	Dettingen Way	4 Lentara Court
Milwaukee, WI 53213	Bury St Edmunds, Suffolk, IP33 3YB	Cheltenham, Victoria, 3192 Australia
Email: info@halleonard.com	Email: info@halleonardeurope.com	Email: info@halleonard.com.au

Acknowledgements

© 2021 by RSL Awards Ltd. and Hal Leonard Europe Ltd.
All Rights Reserved
Catalogue Number: RSK200148
ISBN: 978-1-78936-293-0
18 Nov 2022 | Errata details can be found at www.rslawards.com/errata

2021 Syllabus
Syllabus Designers: Jono Harrison and Eva Brandt
Syllabus Director: Tim Bennett-Hart
Syllabus Consultants: Eva Brandt, Samantha Richards, Sarah Page, Jamie Spencer, Abbie Thomas
Syllabus Advisors: Dr. Andrew McBirnie, Stuart Slater, Tim Bennett-Hart, Daniel Francis, Simon Troup

2021 Publishing
Compiled and edited by Jono Harrison and Eva Brandt
Internal design and layout by Simon Troup (Digital Music Art)
Music engraving by Simon Troup (Digital Music Art)
Cover designed by Phillip Millard (Rather Nice Design)
Cover updates by Neil Hart and Simon Troup
Fact Files written by Abbie Thomas and Oliver Goss
Performance Notes written by Eva Brandt
Proofreading by Eva Brandt, Oliver Goss and Jennie Troup
Cover photography © Kevin Mazur for Getty Images
   (Billie Eilish and Finneas O'Connell, 2021)
Vocal and piano arrangements by Jono Harrison, Andy Robertson and Hal Leonard LLC

2021 Audio
Produced by Jono Harrison, Rory Harvey, Pete Riley, Stefan Mehandra and Katie Hector

2021 Musicians
Katie Hector, Katie Virgoe and Stefan Mehandra – Vocals
Jono Harrison – Piano, keys, guitar
Rory Harvey – Guitar, keys, bass, programming
Pete Riley – Drums and percussion

Executive Producers
Norton York, John Simpson and Suzanne Harlow

Distribution
Exclusive Distributors: Hal Leonard

Contacting RSL Awards
www.rslawards.com
Telephone: +44 (0)345 460 4747
Email: info@rslawards.com

2014 Syllabus Content
Syllabus design and production: James Uings, Simon Troup, Stephen Lawson, Stuart Slater
Vocal specialists and consultants: Martin Hibbert, Eva Brandt, Emily Nash, Stuart Slater, Sarah Page
Full transcriptions and backing tracks by Hal Leonard LLC
Supporting tests composition: Martin Hibbert, James Uings, Jon Musgrave, Jodie Davies, Ryan Moore, Chris Hawkins, Jonathan Preiss, Lucie Burns (Lazy Hammock)
Supporting tests recorded, mixed and mastered by Duncan Jordan (Langlei Studios)
Additional supporting test backing tracks recorded by Jon Musgrave and Jon Bishop
Musicians: Neal Andrews, Lucie Burns (Lazy Hammock), Jodie Davies, Tenisha Edwards, Noam Lederman, Beth Loates-Taylor, Dave Marks, Salena Mastroianni, Paul Miro, Ryan Moore, Jon Musgrave, Chris Smart, Ross Stanley, T-Jay, Stacy Taylor, Daniel Walker

Table of Contents

Introductions & Information

- 1 Title Page
- 2 Acknowledgements
- 3 Table of Contents
- 4 Welcome to Rockschool Vocals Grade 1
- 6 Repertoire Overview

Hit Tunes

- 7 We Will Rock You .... Queen
- 11 Don't Stop the Music .... Rihanna
- 17 A Million Dreams .... from *The Greatest Showman*
- 23 I Love You .... Billie Eilish
- 29 Stand by Me .... Ben E. King
- 33 Fireflies .... Owl City
- 39 How Far I'll Go .... from *Moana*
- 47 Somewhere Only We Know .... Lily Allen
- 53 Friends .... Kelvin Jones
- 59 It Means Beautiful .... from *Everybody's Talking About Jamie*

Technical Exercises

- 65 Scales, Arpeggios, Intervals & Technical Studies

Supporting Tests

- 68 Sight Reading
- 69 Improvisation & Interpretation
- 70 Ear Tests
- 71 General Musicianship Questions

Additional Information

- 72 Pre-Examination Checklist
- 73 Entering Exams, Exam Procedure & Marking Schemes
- 74 Musical Interpretation & Free Choice Pieces
- 75 Copyright Information
- 76 Rockschool Popular Music Theory

Welcome to Rockschool Vocals Grade 1

Welcome to Rockschool Vocals Syllabus 2021. This book and accompanying downloadable audio contain everything you need to sing at Grade 1.

Vocals Exams
At each grade you have the option of taking one of two different types of examination:

- **Grade Exam**
  A Grade Exam is a mixture of music performances, technical work and tests. You prepare three pieces (two of which may be Free Choice Pieces) and the contents of the Technical Exercise section. This accounts for 75% of the exam marks. The other 25% consists of: either a Sight Reading or an Improvisation & Interpretation test (10%), two Ear Tests (10%), and finally you will be asked five General Musicianship Questions (5%). The pass mark is 60%.

- **Performance Certificate**
  In a Performance Certificate you sing five pieces. Up to three of these can be Free Choice Pieces. Each song is marked out of 20 and the pass mark is 60%.

Book Contents
This book is divided into a number of sections. These are:

- **Exam Pieces**
  Ten popular songs covering a breadth of contemporary musical styles, arranged for the grade level. At the beginning of the book there is a Repertoire Overview page outlining the key, tempo, genre and melodic range of the song, as well as a summary of the main technical and stylistic features to implement.

  Each score is preceded by background information about the original recording and performing artist, and this is followed by expanded performance notes giving further guidance on approaching the songs.

  The scores are notated as top line vocal parts with lyrics, chord symbols and backing vocal references where helpful. The notation also includes professionally-arranged piano accompaniments for teaching, audition and performance purposes.

  In addition to the book notation, there is also a separate vocal-only digital score included in your downloads for extra ease of use.

- **Technical Exercises**
  A selection of scales, arpeggios, intervals and technical studies must be performed in the exam. Depending on the exercise, you may see an example (with a range of optional starting notes), or a choice between exercises (to suit your vocal range). There is a pre-examination checklist at the back of the book, where you can note your choices of starting notes and examples ahead of the examination.

- **Supporting Tests**
  Firstly, you may choose *either* a Sight Reading *or* an Improvisation & Interpretation test. These tests are previously unseen and examples are given in the book. You will then need to respond to two Ear Tests focusing on melodic and rhythmic recall. You will also be asked a set of General Musicianship Questions (GMQs) at the end of the exam. Examples of the types of tests likely to appear in the exam are printed in this book.

- **General Information**
  Finally, you will find information on exam procedures, including online examination entry, marking schemes, your pre-exam checklist, and information on Free Choice Pieces and improvisation requirements for each grade.

Audio
Each song in Vocals Grade 1 has two audio tracks.

These are:

- A full track, featuring a professional vocalist's stylistic interpretation of the score. This can be helpful for further ideas beyond the original recorded version.

- A backing track with the vocal removed so you can sing along with the band or piano. The backing tracks should be used in examinations. There are also audio examples of the supporting tests printed in the book.

There are also example recordings and backing tracks included as part of your download for the technical exercises and supporting test sections.

In hardcopy books, all accompanying audio can be downloaded using the unique download code and URL found on the title page (page 1) of the book. In digital editions the audio is included in the download.

The audio files are supplied in MP3 format. Once downloaded you will be able to play them on any compatible device.

All candidates should read the accompanying syllabus guide when using this grade book. This can be downloaded from the RSL website: *www.rslawards.com*

Repertoire Overview

Song/Artist	Key & Range	Info	Key Features to Implement at this Grade
We Will Rock You Queen		Genre: Rock Key: E minor Tempo: ♩=80 Range: E3 to A4	• Confident chest voice management with breath support • Secure rhythmic phrasing of the melody line • Dynamic variation between verses and chorus • Clarity of the diction and articulation of the lyrics
Don't Stop the Music Rihanna		Genre: Dance-Pop Key: F♯ minor Tempo: ♩=115 Range: A3 to A4	• Managing pitch and intonation in chest and head voice • Secure rhythmic phrasing to the backing track • Including dynamic variation in performance • Confident and clear diction and articulation
A Million Dreams from *The Greatest Showman*		Genre: Musical Theatre Key: E♭ major Tempo: ♩=148 Range: G3 to C5	• Maintaining a suitable tone across the registers • Secure rhythmic and melodic management • Confident management of dynamic changes between sections • Strong communication and articulation of the lyrics
I Love You Billie Eilish		Genre: Pop Key: C major Tempo: ♩=69 Range: G3 to A4 (†)	• Secure control of tone colour and intonation • *Legato* phrasing and dynamic variation • Ability to support longer notes and phrases • Clarity of the diction
Stand by Me Ben E. King		Genre: Soul Key: A major Tempo: ♩=118 Range: A3 to A4 (†)	• Managing registers changes and *falsetto*/head voice • Secure rhythmic and melodic phrasing • Confident dynamic changes between sections • Strong communication and articulation of the lyrics
Fireflies Owl City		Genre: Synth-pop Key: E♭ major Tempo: ♩=90 Range: B♭3 to B♭4 (†)	• Confident management of chest voice and *falsetto* • Rhythmic phrasing with secure pitching • *Staccato* and *legato* phrasing • Strong clarity of articulation and diction
It Means Beautiful from *Everybody's Talking About Jamie*		Genre: Musical Theatre Key: F♯ minor Tempo: ♩=89 Range: F♯3 to C♯5	• Competent management of chest and head voice • Secure rhythmic and melodic detailing • Confident breath support on phrases • Clarity and communication of lyrical content
How Far I'll Go from *Moana*		Genre: Soundtrack Key: E major Tempo: Moderately Range: B3 to D5	• Maintaining a suitable tone across the registers • Secure melodic detailing and pitching • Ability to manage longer notes and phrases • Engaged articulation of the lyrics
Somewhere Only We Know Lily Allen		Genre: Pop Key: B♭ major Tempo: ♩=84 Range: B♭3 to B♭4	• Managing pitch and intonation in chest and head voice • Secure rhythmic phrasing to the backing track • Maintaining breath support on longer phrasing • Clear and confident diction and articulation of the lyrics
Friends Kelvin Jones		Genre: Pop Key: G major Tempo: ♩=110 Range: D3 to E4 (†)	• Managing tone in the upper chest voice and transition • Secure phrasing with *staccato* and accents • Ability to manage longer phrases with breath support • Clarity and expression of the lyrics

† *Range and notation in this table is displayed at actual pitch. The associated score is notated one octave higher than it sounds for legibility.*

We Will Rock You | Queen

Album: *News of the World*
Released: 1977
Label: EMI/Elektra

Genre: Rock
Written by: Brian May
Produced by: Queen and Mike Stone

Background Info

'We Will Rock You' was a worldwide hit for British rock band Queen, and features on their sixth studio album *News of the World*. The track was written by the band's lead guitarist Brian May, who also had songwriting success with hits such as 'Hammer To Fall' and 'Tie Your Mother Down'. 'We Will Rock You' famously begins by using stomps and claps to keep the beat, encouraging audience participation during live performances. Queen were a global phenomenon who are regarded to have had a profound influence on rock music. Their ability to blend genres such as funk, disco and jazz with classic rock brought them worldwide acclaim and saw them inducted into the Rock and Roll Hall of Fame. With frontman Freddie Mercury, the band released over ten studio albums (including posthumous recordings) and became one of the best selling artists of all time.

Performance Notes

In this iconic rock song from the early '80s we hear Freddie Mercury's powerful and theatrical performance.

When learning the song it would be a good idea to break the verses into smaller chunks, clapping the rhythm while slowing down the tempo, before you start applying lyrics and melody.

You should aim to sing with a projected and strong tone quality in your chest voice and this will be easier to maintain if you apply consistent breath support on the phrasing. You can look for an assertive 'speech style' tone quality; as if you had an important message to deliver to a friend or a group of people.

Finally, take your time to learn the lyrics so you can sing these with clear articulation, and look also to include dynamic variation that supports the changes between the verses and chorus for dramatic effect, as heard in the original recording.

'Key Features to Implement at this Grade' are shown in the *Repertoire Overview* on page 6.

We Will Rock You

Words and Music by Brian May

Queen

3.
We will, we will rock you.
11
C
We will, we will rock you.
A G A G A
13
D A D A
16
Asus4 D A Asus4 A Asus4 A
18
Asus4 A Asus4 A Asus4 A
21

Don't Stop the Music | Rihanna

Album: *Good Girl Gone Bad*
Released: 2007
Label: Def Jam/SRP

Genre: Dance-Pop
Written by: Tor Erik Hermansen, Frankie Storm, Mikkel Eriksen and Michael Jackson
Produced by: StarGate

Background Info

'Don't Stop the Music' is a song released by singer Rihanna. The track features on her third studio album *Good Girl Gone Bad*, and proved popular worldwide. The song topped the charts in several countries, and was certified 4x platinum in the US where it sold over 4 million copies.

Rihanna started releasing music in 2003 after she was discovered in her home country of Barbados. She then auditioned and was signed to Jay-Z's record label Def Jam in 2005. Rihanna has released eight studio albums, four of which have gone on to top the UK Album Chart. The singer has collaborated with many famous artists, including Kanye West, Eminem, Paul McCartney and Jay-Z. She has received nine Grammys, and holds six Guinness World Records.

Performance Notes

This up-tempo pop song demonstrates Rihanna's ability to create a vibrant and resonant tone colour, particularly in her chest voice.

You don't have to copy her tone quality; however, you should aim for a 'forward placement' of the tone, which means to direct/create resonance that vibrates in the harder and 'brighter' parts of the vocal tract. This positioning can help to produce a more contemporary vocal sound.

Aim to be rhythmically secure throughout with a confident entry on the lyrics 'Please don't stop the music'. You could add accents (stronger attacks) on the quarter notes in the chorus for dynamic emphasis on these words. In the pre-chorus make sure the melodic detailing of the note pitches and intonation is secure.

The lyrical content of the song calls for engaged communication and some demonstration of dynamic changes, particularly between the chorus and verses.

'Key Features to Implement at this Grade' are shown in the ***Repertoire Overview*** on page 6.

Don't Stop the Music

Words and Music by Tor Erik Hermansen, Frankie Storm, Mikkel Eriksen and Michael Jackson

Rihanna

Copyright © 2007 EMI Music Publishing Ltd., Sony Music Publishing LLC, Dabney Music Publishing, Sony Music Publishing UK Limited and Mijac Music
All Rights Administered by Sony Music Publishing LLC, 424 Church Street, Suite 1200, Nashville, TN 37219
International Copyright Secured   All Rights Reserved
- contains a sample of "Wanna Be Startin' Something" by Michael Jackson

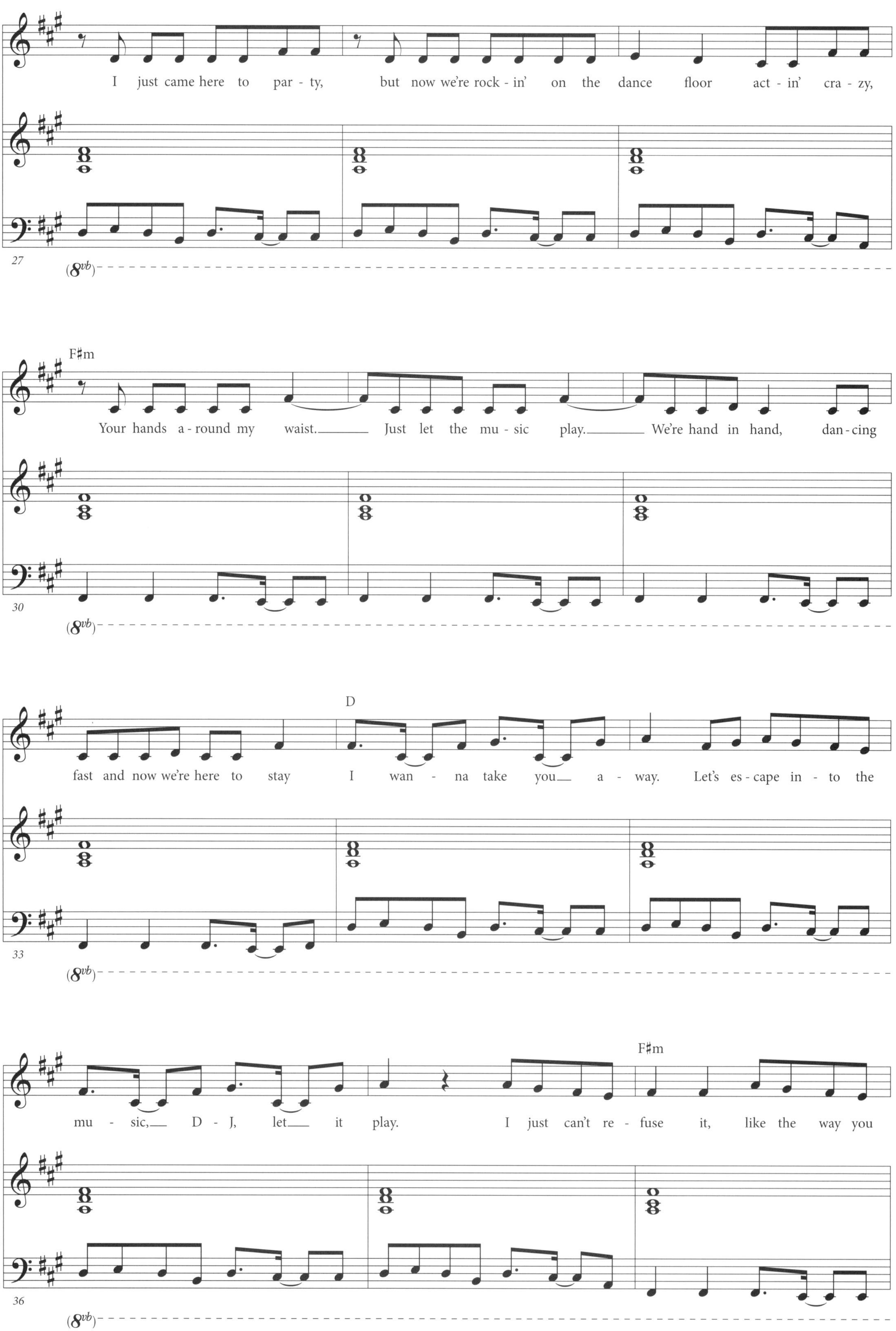

A Million Dreams | from *The Greatest Showman*

Album: *The Greatest Showman: Original Motion Picture Soundtrack*
Released: 2017
Label: Atlantic

Genre: Musical Theatre
Written by: Benj Pasek and Justin Paul
Produced by: Joseph Trapanese, Justin Paul and Alex Lacamoire

Background Info

'A Million Dreams' was written for the 2017 musical film *The Greatest Showman*. The song was performed by Ziv Zaifman, Hugh Jackman and Michelle Williams, and featured on the film's official soundtrack. Originally written for three singers, the arrangement for this performance piece has been written for a solo vocalist.

Although 'A Million Dreams' wasn't released as an official single, its popularity among listeners has led to several cover versions/renditions being released by famous musicians, including Susan Boyle and Pink.

The film *The Greatest Showman* was a great commercial success, and grossed an income of over $435 million worldwide, alongside several award nominations, including Best Original Song for 'This Is Me' at the 2018 Golden Globes.

Performance Notes

This popular song from 'The Greatest Showman' is an opportunity for anyone keen on the film score genre to tell a convincing story with a strong emphasis on the communication of the lyrics.

The original recording features three different voices, but this abridged version has been arranged in the key of E♭ to offer better positioning for a solo vocal performance. You may still prefer to perform the song in a different key, to suit your voice type and to allow you to comfortably reach the top notes with a clear and consistent tone quality. Note that for this grade, the last phrase (from bar 56) may be sung in either octave.

Notice how the melody requires you to be confident with your rhythmic phrasing, with some accented notes and emphasis on the enunciation and positioning of words. You should also try varying your dynamics in order to demonstrate communication and expression of the lyrical content.

'Key Features to Implement at this Grade' are shown in the *Repertoire Overview* on page 6.

A Million Dreams

from THE GREATEST SHOWMAN
Words and Music by Benj Pasek and Justin Paul

Ziv Zaifman, Hugh Jackman
and Michelle Williams

I Love You | Billie Eilish

Album: *When We All Fall Asleep, Where Do We Go?*
Released: 2019
Label: Darkroom/Interscope

Genre: Pop
Written by: Billie Eilish O'Connell and Finneas O'Connell
Produced by: Finneas O'Connell

Background Info

'I Love You' is a song by American singer-songwriter Billie Eilish, and features on her debut studio album *When We All Fall Asleep, Where Do We Go?*. The track was co-written by Billie Eilish and her older brother Finneas O'Connell. Although it wasn't released as a single, 'I Love You' received positive reviews and commercial success, becoming certified platinum in the US. After her first singles and EP, Billie Eilish went on to release her first studio album in 2019 to great critical acclaim, and debuted on top of the US Billboard and UK Album Chart. Her distinct singing and musical style has led to her gaining a large and diverse fanbase. Billie Eilish continues to release material today, with her second studio album due to be released in 2021.

Performance Notes

In this beautiful pop ballad from Billie Eilish, we hear her unique tone with its atmospheric breathiness and her ability to manage longer phrases and notes effortlessly.

For this abridged arrangement notice the melody has been written an octave higher than sung and there is an alternative lyric suggestion in bar 12 which you may use if you prefer.

If you choose to opt for a breathier tone quality, you should still use ample support to achieve clarity and secure intonation. Aim to pronounce the words with clear articulation and forward placement for a contemporary sound.

There are great opportunities to apply dynamic variation and expression on the phrases, particularly in the chorus. The *legato* "Mm hmm" phrase into the chorus doesn't leave you much space for taking a breath. You can delay this until later in the phrase, but you will need good breath control to achieve this.

'Key Features to Implement at this Grade' are shown in the *Repertoire Overview* on page 6.

I Love You

Words and Music by Billie Eilish O'Connell and Finneas O'Connell

Billie Eilish

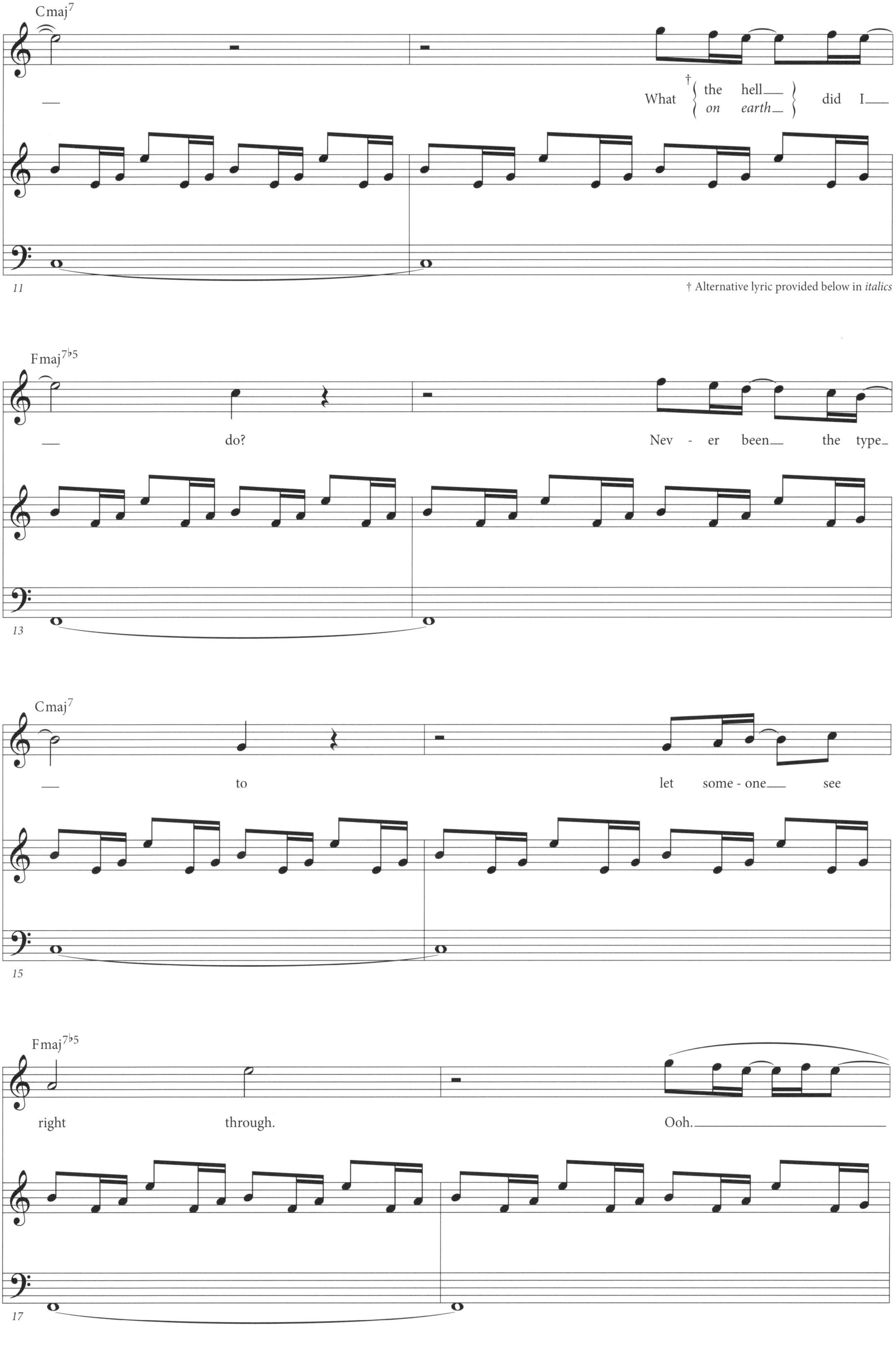
Cmaj7
What † { the hell / on earth } did I
11
† Alternative lyric provided below in *italics*
Fmaj7♭5
do? Nev - er been the type
13
Cmaj7
to let some - one see
15
Fmaj7♭5
right through. Ooh.
17

Stand by Me | Ben E. King

Album: *Don't Play That Song!*
Released: 1961
Label: Atco

Genre: Soul
Written by: Jerry Leiber, Mike Stoller and Ben E. King
Produced by: Jerry Leiber and Mike Stoller

Background Info

'Stand by Me' was a song released by American singer-songwriter Ben E. King. The song was originally released in 1961 and written with songwriting team Jerry Leiber and Mike Stoller, who famously wrote several hits for Elvis Presley in the 1950s. It was later re-released in 1986 for the 25th anniversary of the feature film of the same name. 'Stand by Me' was commercially very successful, reaching number 4 on the US Billboard Hot 100 and achieving Platinum status in the UK. The popularity of 'Stand by Me' has led to hundreds of cover versions, including renditions by Otis Redding, John Lennon and Tracy Chapman..

Ben E. King started his music career in the late 1950s when he joined R&B group The Drifters. He later left the group and went on to release music as a solo artist, leaving a large catalogue of music spanning more than 50 years. His songs during the '50s and '60s remain influential to modern soul music to this day.

Performance Notes

This is an abridged arrangement of Ben E. King's classic soul song from the '60s, and will suit any vocalists looking to explore the upper parts of their chest voice, transition and head voice.

You may need to find a suitable key where you can comfortably reach the top notes with secure intonation. For a convincing tone quality, you can use a 'speech style' approach, making sure the tone in your falsetto/head voice is not too 'breathy' by engaging your resonators and applying breath support.

Showing confidence and understanding of the rhythmic feel is a key element to performing this song, and you should aim for a laid back delivery, while still being securely placed on the beat with the bassline riff. You can look to communicate the lyrical content further by by starting softly and then building up with *crescendos* into the choruses.

'Key Features to Implement at this Grade' are shown in the *Repertoire Overview* on page 6.

Stand by Me

Words and Music by Jerry Leiber, Mike Stoller and Ben E. King

Ben E. King

Note: *Vocal sounds one octave lower than notated throughout*

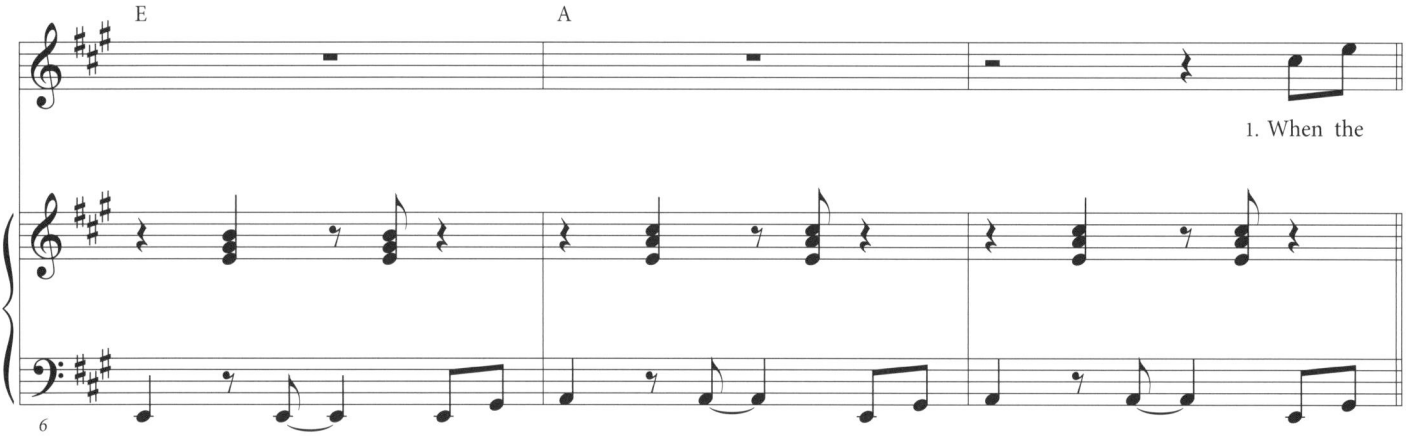

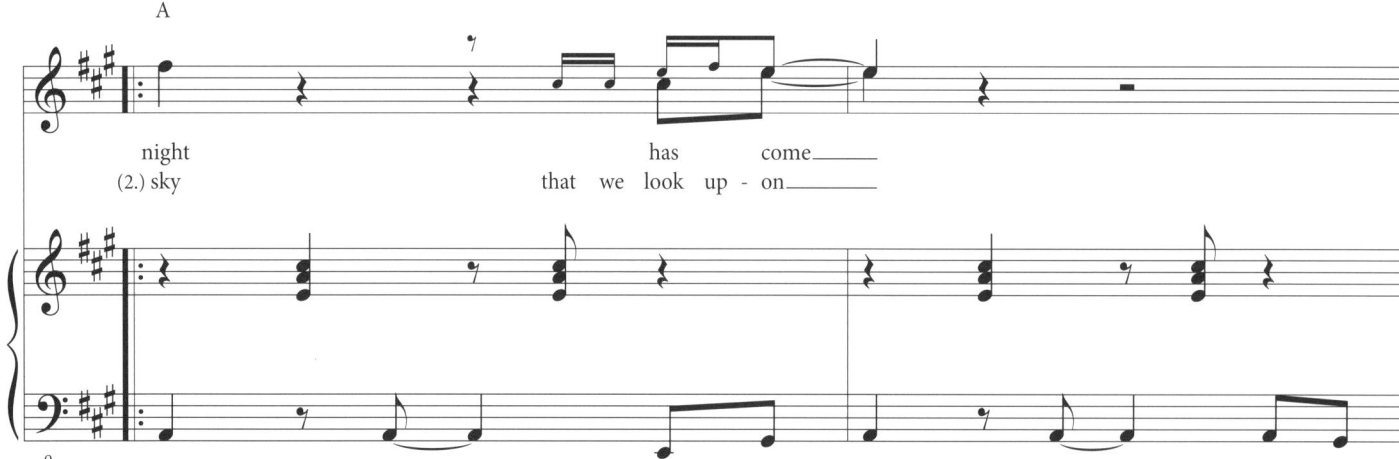

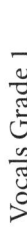

Fireflies | Owl City

Album: *Ocean Eyes*
Released: 2009
Label: Universal Republic

Genre: Synth-Pop
Written by: Adam Young
Produced by: Adam Young and Matt Thiessen

Background Info

'Fireflies' is a song by American electronic music project Owl City. Taken from their second album *Ocean Eyes*, the song topped the charts in several countries worldwide. It was written by Owl City's founding member Adam Young, with featured vocals by Matt Thiessen, a songwriter for American rock band Relient K. The song was met with critical acclaim, and went on to sell over 7 million copies in the US.

Owl City started their career with two online self-releases before finding further global success following a record deal with Universal Republic and releasing *Ocean Eyes*. Founder and creator Adam Young has also had success making film music, and has created songs for animated movies, including *The Croods*, *Wreck-It Ralph* and *The Smurfs 2*. 'Fireflies' remains Owl City's most successful single release.

Performance Notes

This synth-pop tune is a fun challenge for this grade with some complex rhythms and larger intervallic leaps.

You can use the original version to inspire your choice of tone colour, and you should aim to sound consistent in both your chest voice and falsetto with a confident yet soft tone quality.

You should also aim to engage your resonators in your higher range to get a smooth transition and clarity on your top notes. Intonation and pitching of these notes are important and applying breath support will help you achieve this.

There is a range of expressive techniques to implement with the *staccato* phrasing of the melody in the verses to the longer notes in the chorus. You can try over-enunciating the words to explore how it supports the clarity of the articulation of the lyrics as well as the rhythmic synchronisation to the backing track.

'Key Features to Implement at this Grade' are shown in the *Repertoire Overview* on page 6.

Fireflies

Words and Music by Adam Young

Owl City

Note: *Vocal sounds one octave lower than notated throughout*

You would not believe your eyes if ten million fireflies lit up the world as I fell asleep.

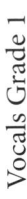

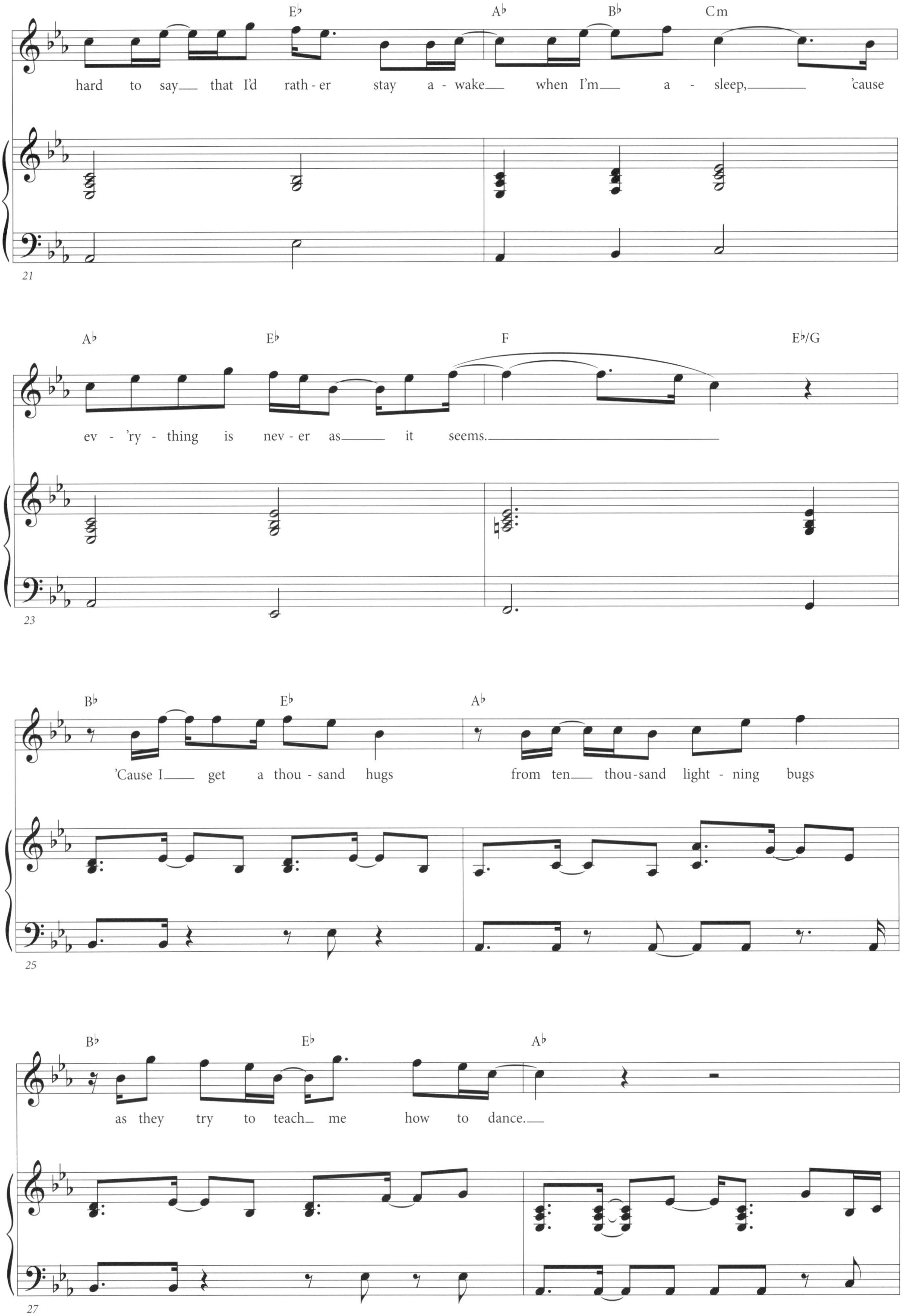
E♭ A♭ B♭ Cm
hard to say that I'd rath-er stay a-wake when I'm a-sleep, 'cause
21
A♭ E♭ F E♭/G
ev-'ry-thing is nev-er as it seems.
23
B♭ E♭ A♭
'Cause I get a thou-sand hugs from ten thou-sand light-ning bugs
25
B♭ E♭ A♭
as they try to teach me how to dance.
27

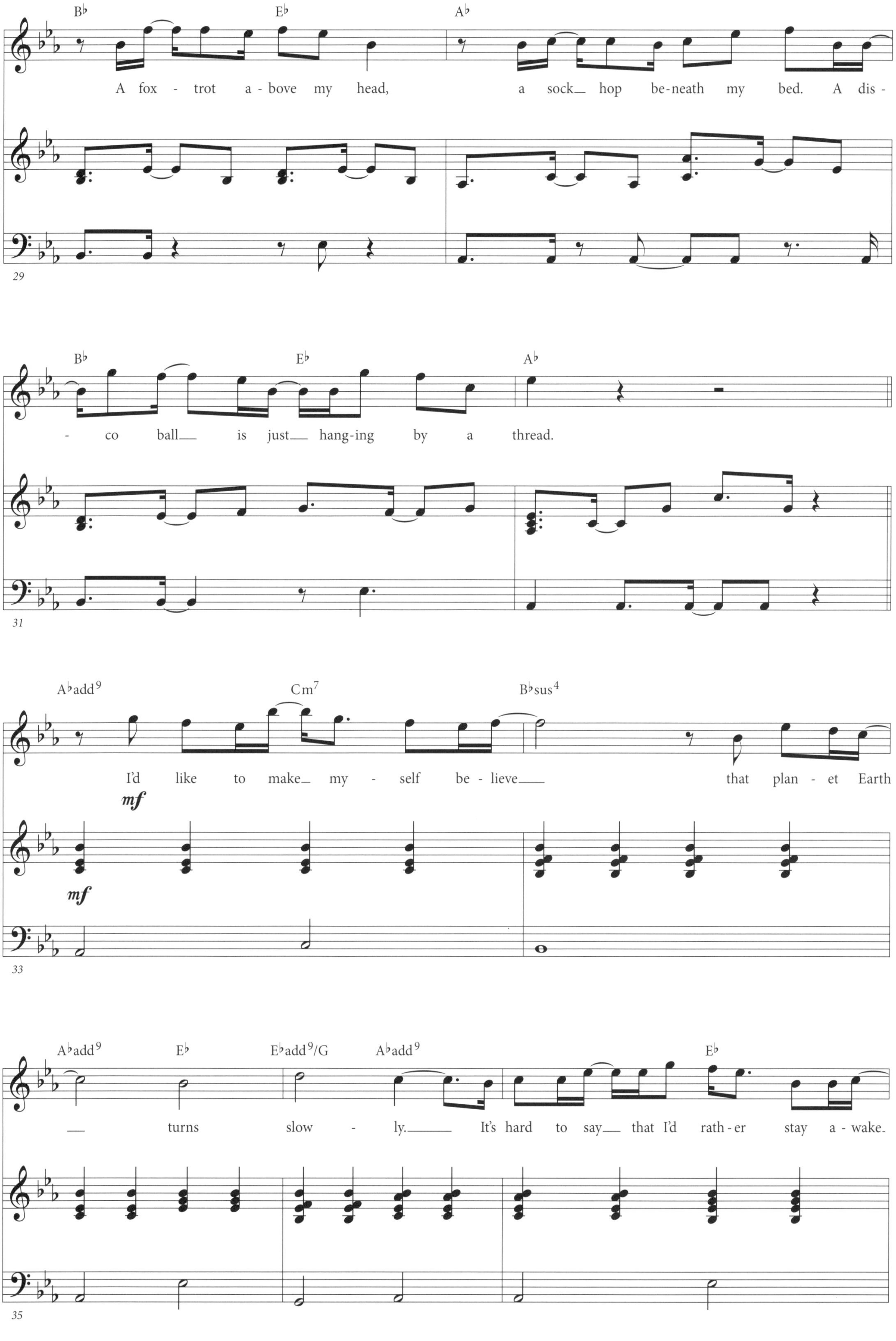
B♭ E♭ A♭
A fox - trot a - bove my head, a sock hop be-neath my bed. A dis -
29
B♭ E♭ A♭
- co ball is just hang-ing by a thread.
31
A♭add9 Cm7 B♭sus4
I'd like to make my - self be - lieve that plan - et Earth
mf
mf
33
A♭add9 E♭ E♭add9/G A♭add9 E♭
turns slow - ly. It's hard to say that I'd rath - er stay a - wake.
35

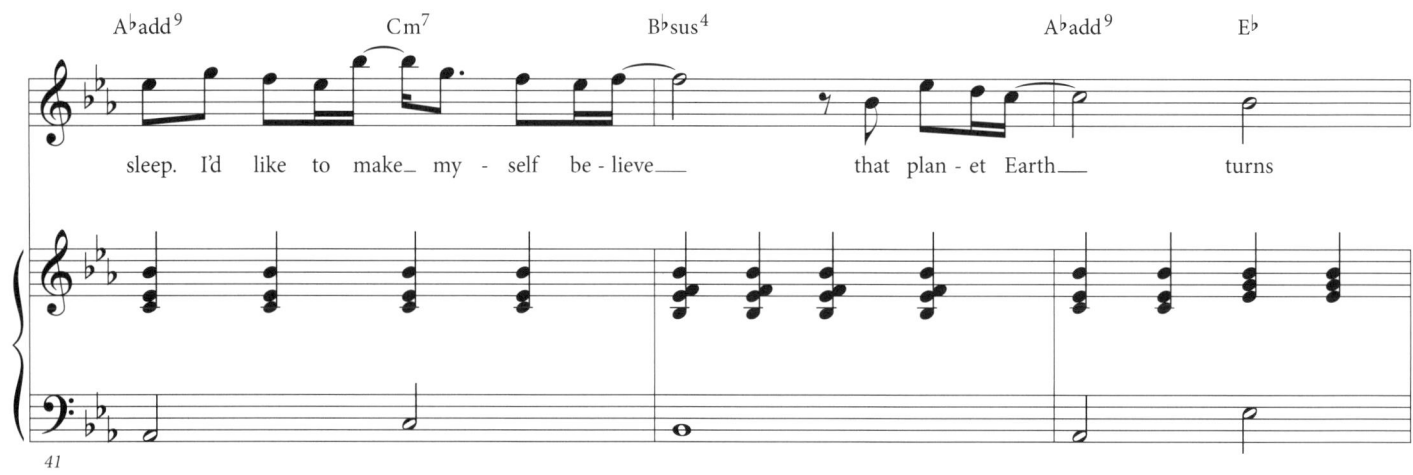

How Far I'll Go | from *Moana*

Album: *Moana: Original Motion Picture Soundtrack*
Released: 2016
Label: Walt Disney Records

Genre: Pop
Written by: Lin-Manuel Miranda
Produced by: Lin-Manuel Miranda

Background Info

'How Far I'll Go' was written for Disney's 2016 animated film *Moana*. The song was performed in the film by actor and singer Auli'i Cravalho, with a separate version of the track performed by Alessia Cara and released as a single. Both versions appear on the 2016 release of *Moana: Original Motion Picture Soundtrack*, which peaked at number 7 on the UK Albums chart.

The popularity of the film and song led to several award nominations, including Best Original Song at the 2017 Academy Awards, and winning Best Song Written for Visual Media at the 2018 Grammy Awards.

Performance Notes

This popular film score song offers a great challenge for anyone keen on the musical theatre genre.

The song has a wide range (B3-D5) and some larger intervallic leaps and you should start by establishing a key where you can comfortably reach the top notes, aiming for these to be sung with a confident tone in your head voice.

Take time to study the melodic detailing for secure intonation and be sure to prepare for the key change (from bar 35) taking the last chorus up a semitone.

You can look to use a speech-style tone quality, as if you are talking directly to someone in conversation. This will help you avoid singing too loud and pushing the upper part of your range. Confident emphasis of the lyrics with clear articulation will help your overall phrasing and communication of the lyrics.

'Key Features to Implement at this Grade' are shown in the *Repertoire Overview* on page 6.

How Far I'll Go

from MOANA
Music and Lyrics by Lin-Manuel Miranda

Auli'i Cravalho

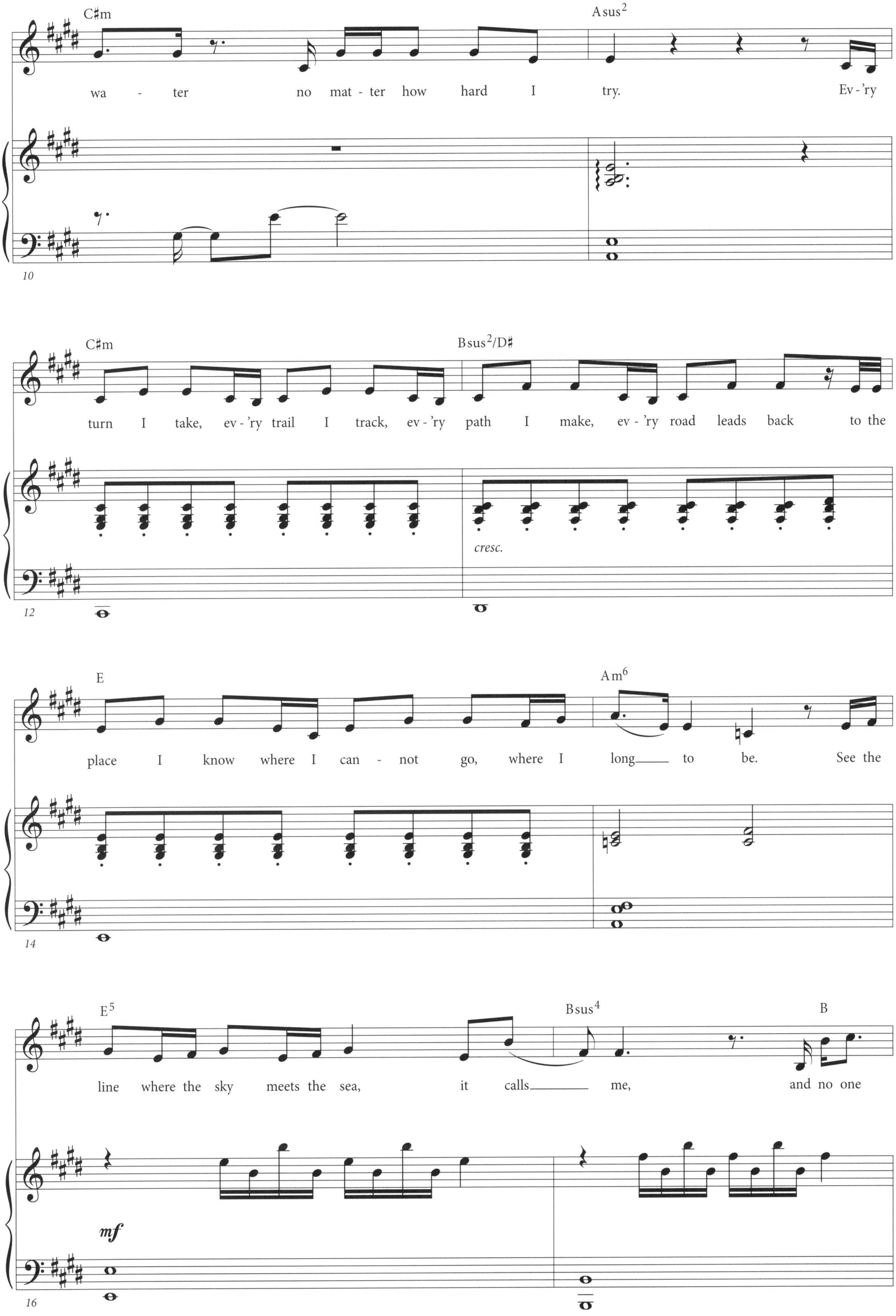
C♯m
Asus2
wa - ter no mat - ter how hard I try. Ev - 'ry
10
C♯m
Bsus2/D♯
turn I take, ev - 'ry trail I track, ev - 'ry path I make, ev - 'ry road leads back to the
cresc.
12
E
Am6
place I know where I can - not go, where I long to be. See the
14
E5
Bsus4
B
line where the sky meets the sea, it calls me, and no one
mf
16

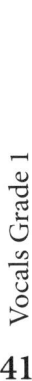

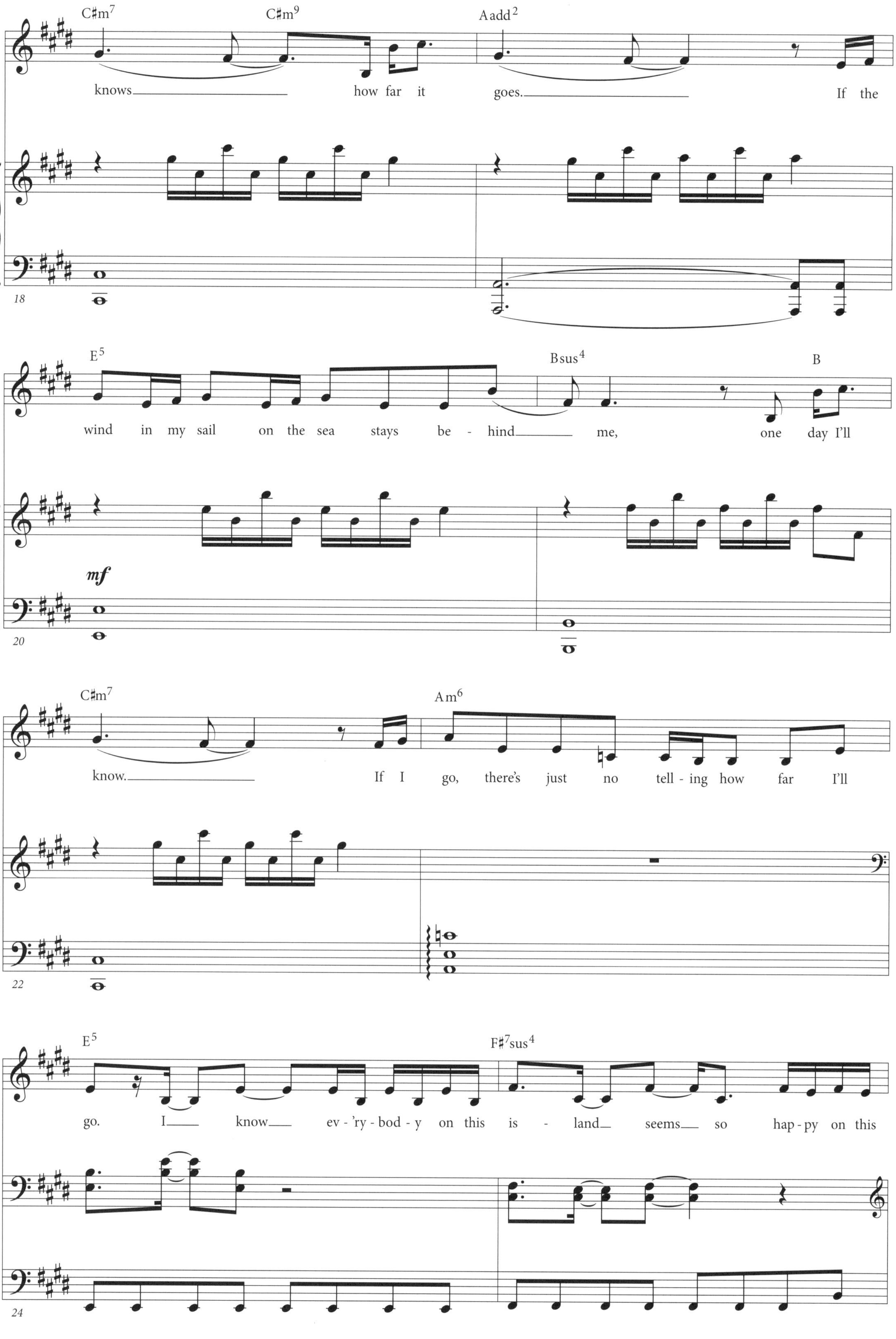
C♯m7 C♯m9 Aadd2
knows how far it goes. If the
18
E5 Bsus4 B
wind in my sail on the sea stays be - hind me, one day I'll
mf
20
C♯m7 Am6
know. If I go, there's just no tell - ing how far I'll
22
E5 F♯7sus4
go. I know ev - 'ry - bod - y on this is - land seems so hap - py on this
24

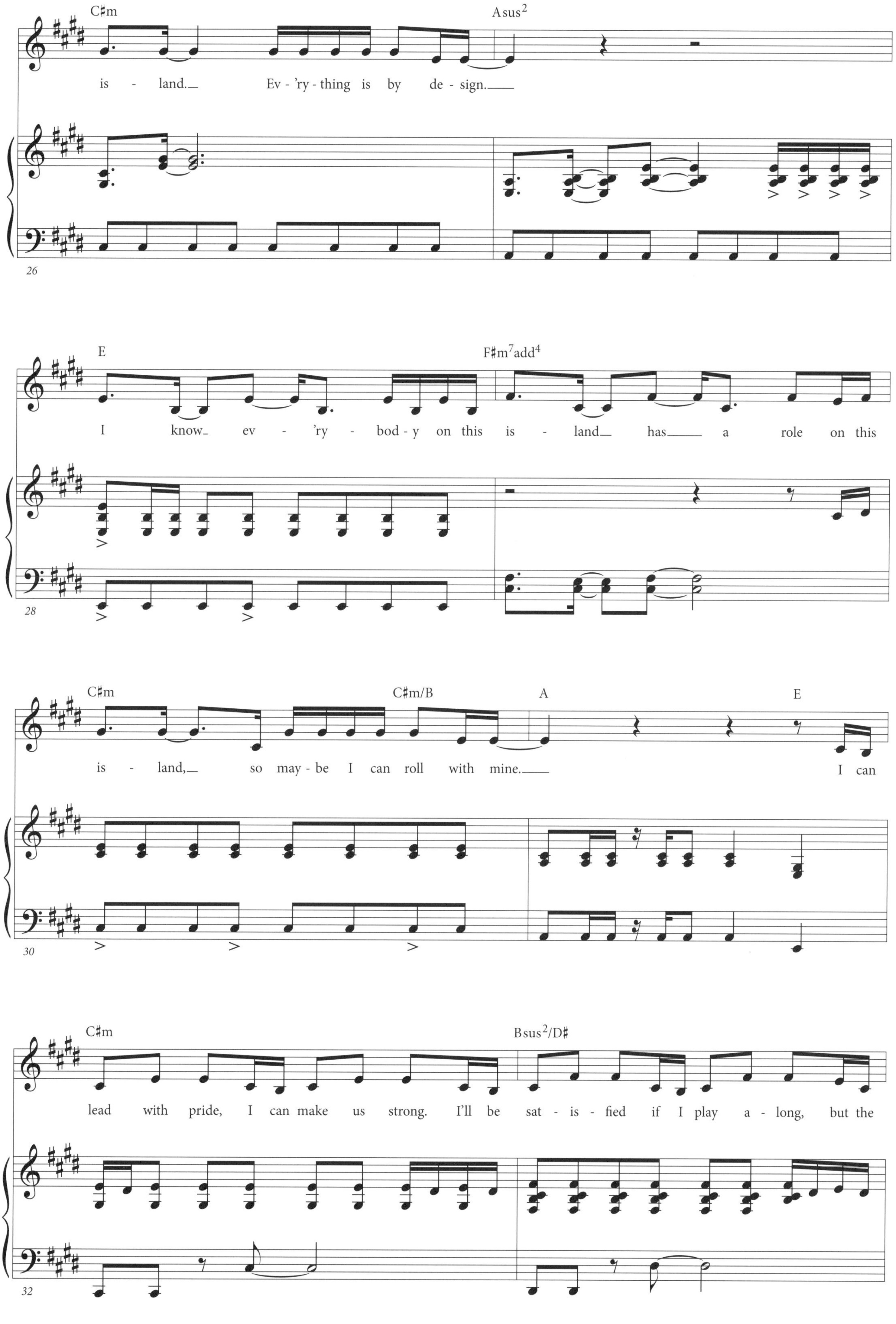
C♯m
Asus2
is - land. Ev - 'ry - thing is by de - sign.
26
E
F♯m7add4
I know ev - 'ry - bod - y on this is - land has a role on this
28
C♯m
C♯m/B
A
E
is - land, so may - be I can roll with mine. I can
30
C♯m
Bsus2/D♯
lead with pride, I can make us strong. I'll be sat - is - fied if I play a - long, but the
32

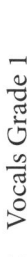

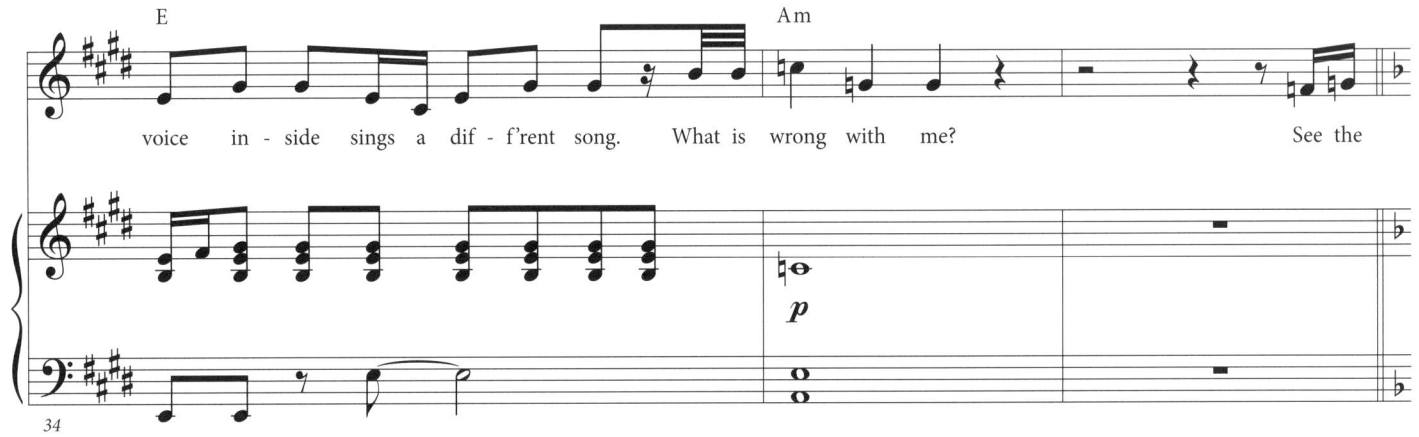

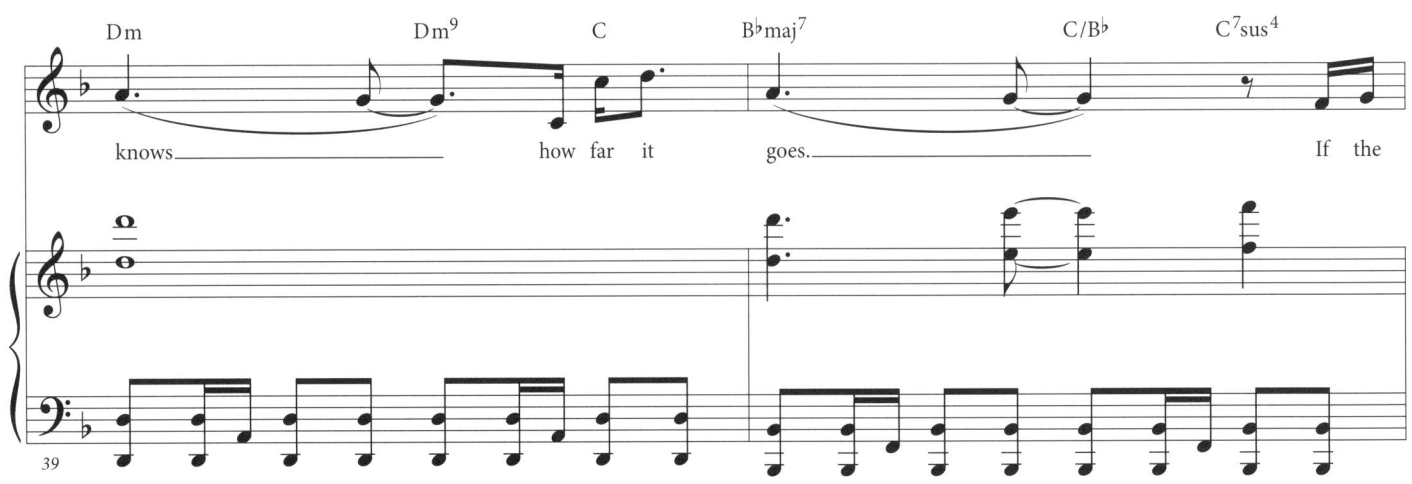

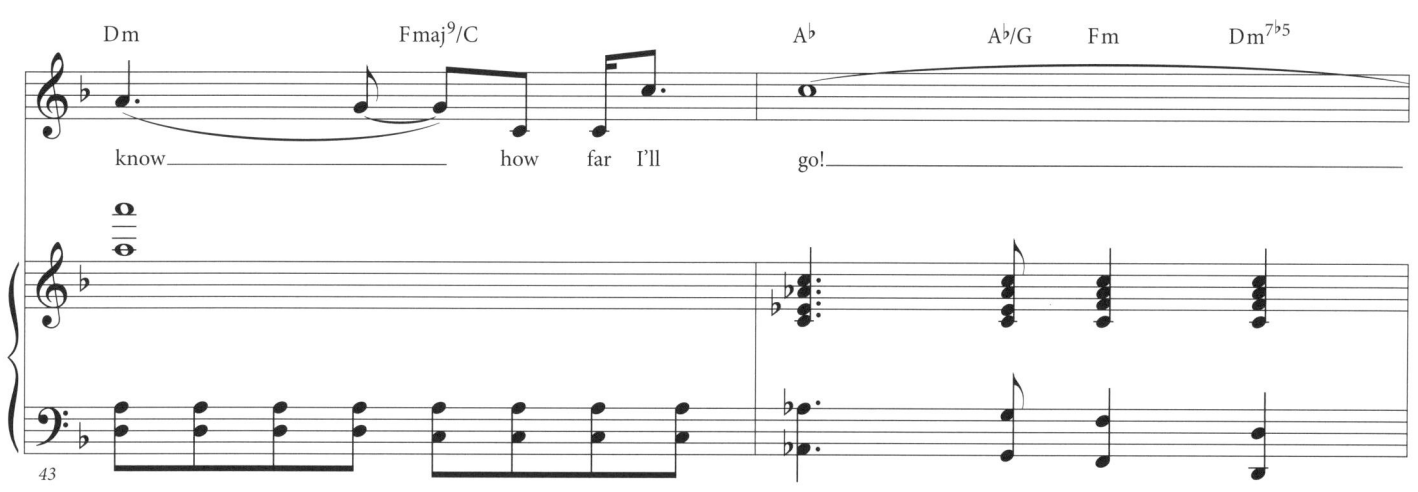

Somewhere Only We Know | Lily Allen

Album: *Sheezus*
Released: 2013
Label: Regal/Parlophone

Genre: Pop
Written by: Tim Rice-Oxley, Richard Hughes and Tom Chaplin
Produced by: Paul Beard

Background Info

'Somewhere Only We Know' was a song originally released in 2004 by British rock band Keane. The success and popularity of the song led to several cover versions, including a cover in 2013 by Lily Allen. Lily Allen's version was featured on a John Lewis Christmas advert and became her third number 1 single.

Lily Allen gained popularity after uploading her music to the social networking site MySpace, leading to mainstream success when her debut single 'Smile' peaked at number one in the UK. She has since released four studio albums, and has sold more than 5 million records worldwide.

Performance Notes

Originally written and recorded by Keane, this pop/rock ballad was reimagined by Lily Allen and is suitable for both male and female candidates.

In this arrangement you will be performing two verses and a chorus, and this is an opportunity to show how you manage the shift from chest into lower head voice or mix quality. You should work towards an even and secure vocal tone with clear rhythmic phrasing throughout, and this could be supported with a *crescendo* into the chorus.

Confidence in articulation and communication of the lyrics is another key element that you should look to maintain and the melody has some longer phrases that will require you to engage breath support to manage these. Practise the rhythmic phrasing to the backing track with a steady pulse, and watch out for the change of time signature in bar 25.

'Key Features to Implement at this Grade' are shown in the *Repertoire Overview* on page 6.

Somewhere Only We Know

Words and Music by Tim Rice-Oxley, Richard Hughes and Tom Chaplin

Lily Allen

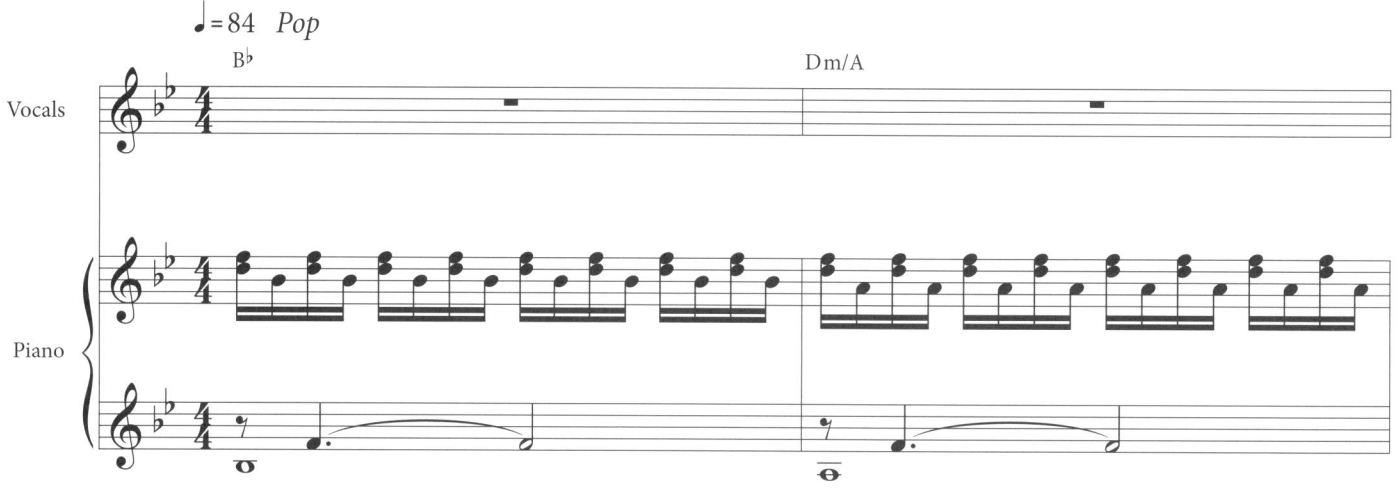

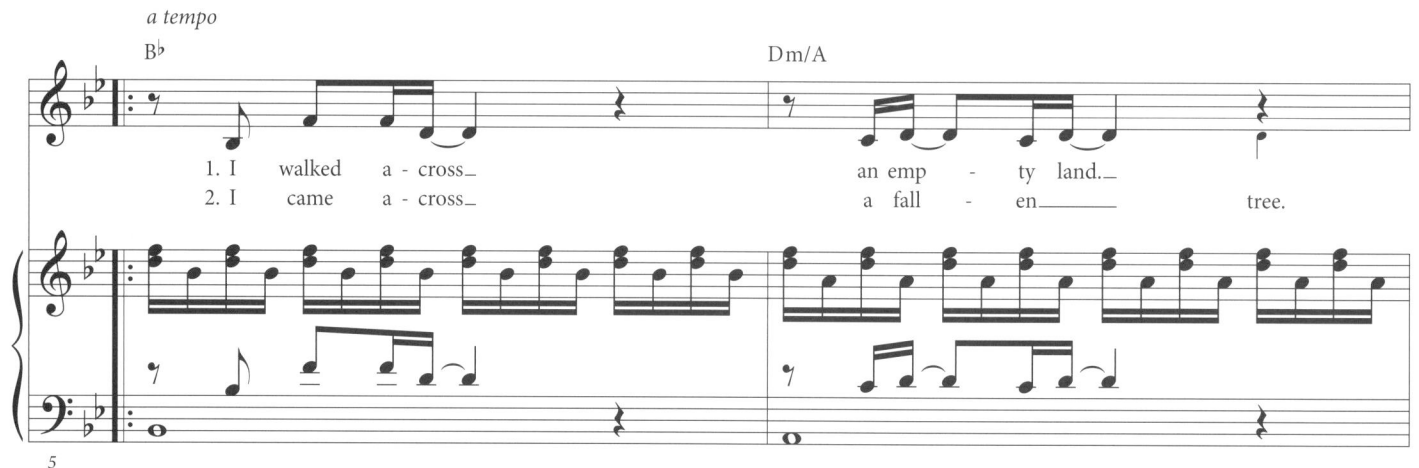

Copyright © 2004 by Universal Music Publishing MGB Ltd.
All Rights in the United States Administered by Universal Music - Careers
International Copyright Secured   All Rights Reserved

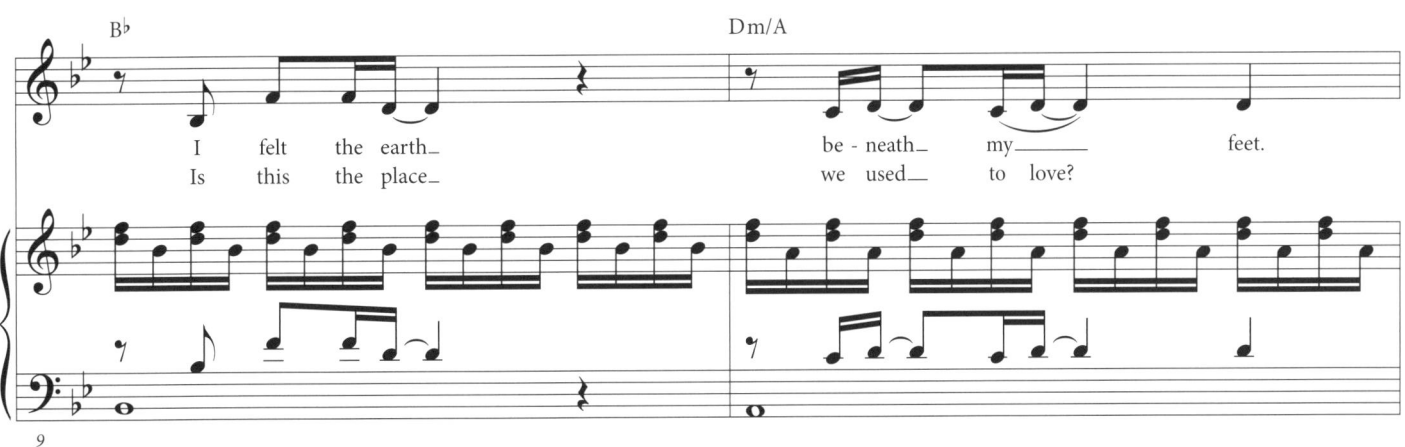
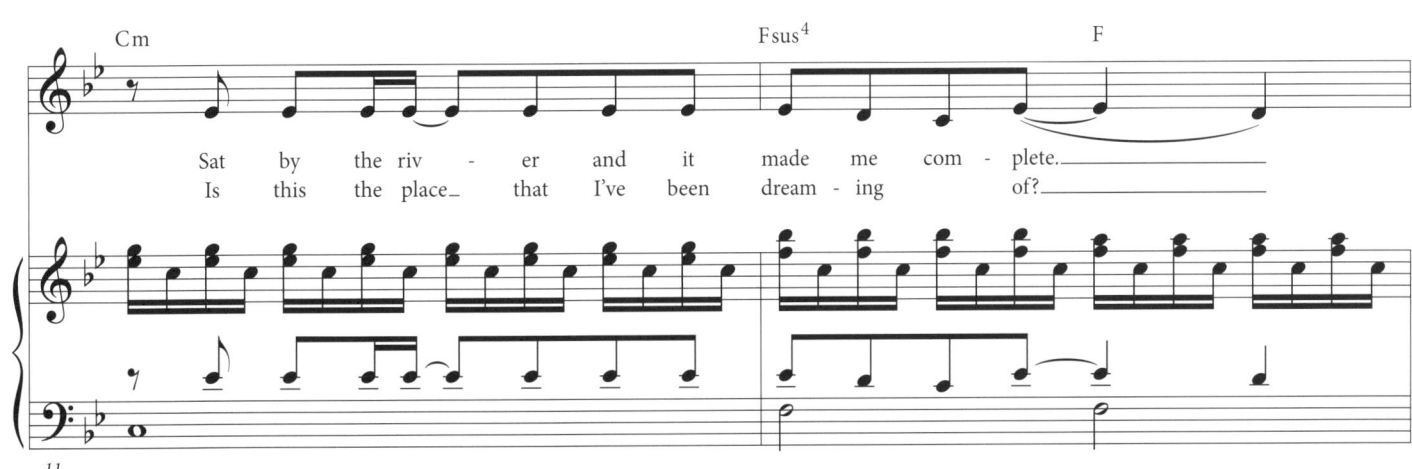

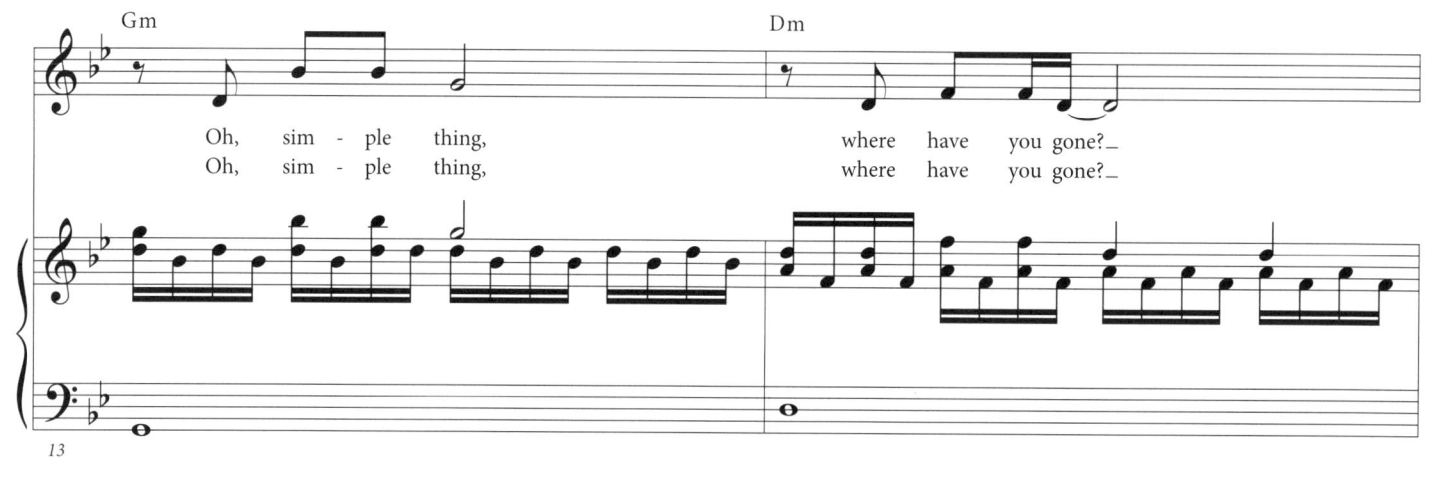

Friends | Kelvin Jones

Released: 2020
Label: Universal

Genre: Pop
Written by: Tinashe Mupani, Alexander Tidebrink and Lucas Riemenschneider

Background Info

'Friends' is a song by British-Zimbabwean singer Kelvin Jones, and was released as a digital single in 2020.

Kelvin Jones first achieved success in 2014 with his debut single 'Call You Home'. The song went viral after being uploaded online, receiving millions of views on YouTube and eventually leading to Kelvin being signed by Sony. Jones has recently supported major UK acts, including James Morrison and KT Tunstall, and continues to release new music.

Performance Notes

This up-tempo pop song from UK singer-songwriter Kelvin Jones is a fun challenge for a singer looking to explore the upper parts of their chest voice and transition.

The overall range of the song is just over an octave and you should aim for the main part to sit comfortably in the upper part of your chest voice. You will need to think about your breath support on the longer phrases, particularly in the pre-chorus, in order to maintain clarity of the tone and accuracy of intonation.

The rhythmic feel is important too, and may be emphasised by *staccato* phrasing on the triplet eighth-notes in the verse and the accented notes in the chorus where the lyrics say 'I, I, I, I'.

Finally, aim for the upbeat message of the song lyrics to be portrayed with strong communication and expression.

'Key Features to Implement at this Grade' are shown in the *Repertoire Overview* on page 6.

Friends

Words and Music by Tinashe Mupani, Alexander Tidebrink and Lucas Riemenschneider

Kelvin Jones

Note: *Vocal sounds one octave lower than notated throughout*

Re-mem-ber when we skipped out of math to be free

and stayed out 'til the dawn?

Talk-ing for hours, rid-ing our skate-boards in our

Copyright © 2020 Budde Music UK Ltd., Budde Music, Inc., Universal Music Publishing AB and Edition Tanzdichgluecklich
All Rights for Budde Music UK Ltd. and Budde Music, Inc. Administered by Downtown DLJ Songs
All Rights for Universal Music Publishing AB Administered by Universal - PolyGram International Tunes, Inc.
All Rights for Edition Tanzdichgluecklich Administered by Universal Music Publishing GmbH
All Rights Reserved   Used by Permission

C Em D Am Bm
yeah you know that we made it. Oh, oh
27
C Em D G Em C Em D
I, I, I, I, we fin-al-ly made it. I, I, I, I,
29
Am Bm C Em D G Em
you know that we made it. I, I, I, I, we fin-al-ly made it.
32
C Em D Am Bm
You know, I know, they know we fin-al-ly made it.
35

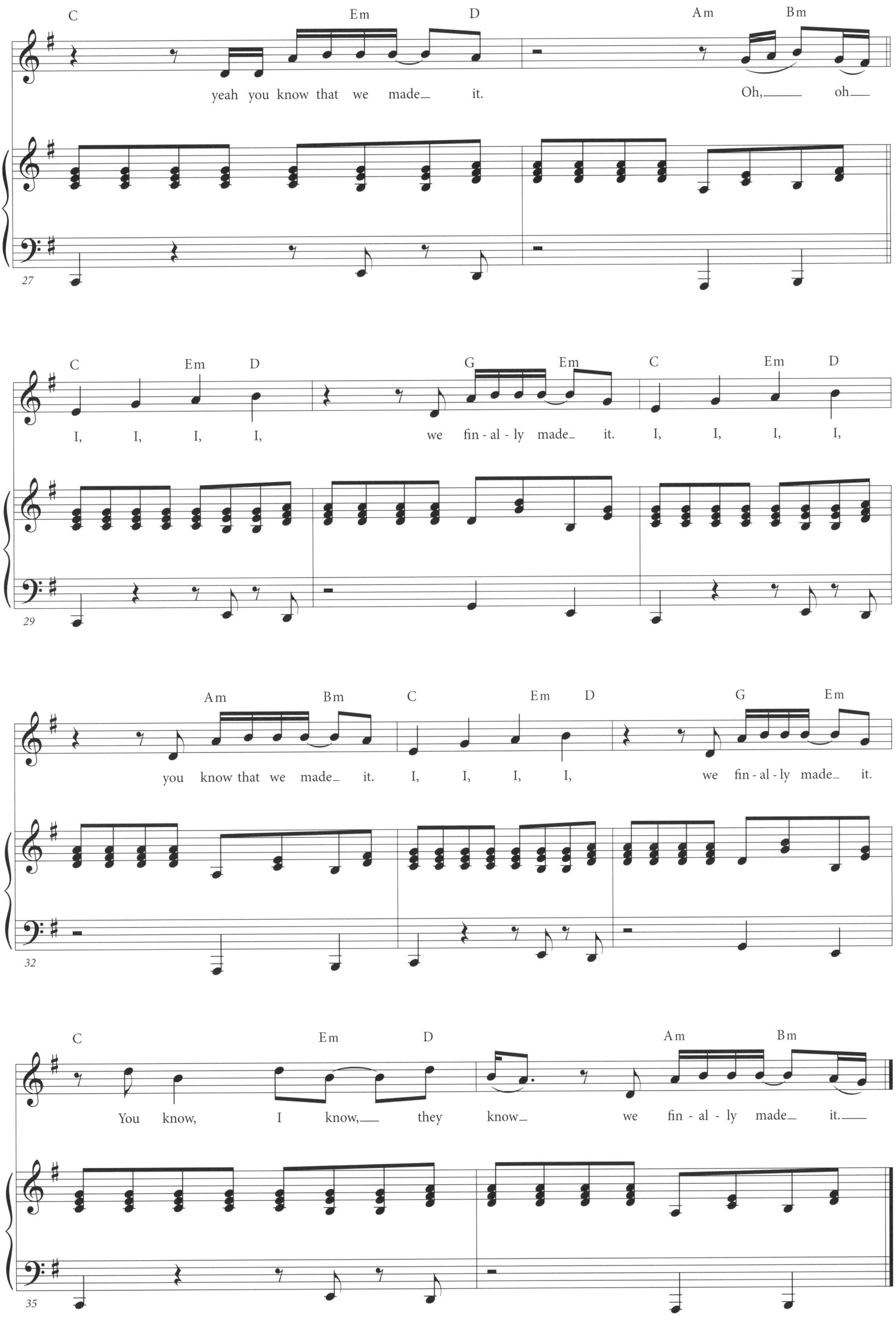

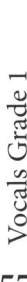

It Means Beautiful | from *Everybody's Talking About Jamie*

Album: *Everybody's Talking About Jamie* (The Concept Album)
Released: 2017
Label: Wilton Way Records
Genre: Musical Theatre
Written by: Daniel Sells and Tom MacRae

Background Info

'It Means Beautiful' was written for the musical *Everybody's Talking About Jamie*. This performance piece is based on a version performed by British actor and singer Courtney Brown, who was featured on a professionally filmed version of the musical released to cinemas in 2018. The song is performed by main character Pritti, who tells Jamie that his name means 'beautiful' in Arabic.

Everybody's Talking About Jamie first premiered in 2017 at Sheffield's Crucible Theatre. Inspired by the 2011 TV documentary *Jamie: Drag Queen at 16*, the musical has gained popularity internationally, and is performed worldwide. It has received several award nominations, including Best New Musical at the Laurence Olivier Awards in 2018. A feature film version of the musical is due to be released in 2021.

Performance Notes

This powerful ballad from the British musical theatre show 'Everybody's talking about Jamie' has a strong lyrical message about self-belief and overcoming prejudice.

A convincing tone quality would be for your chest voice to sound well-supported with a soft yet clear and supported tone, also on the lower notes. You could seek for a similar tone colour in your head voice and it may help you to engage your mouth resonators to not sound too breathy here.

Take some time to study the finer detailing of the rhythmic and melodic features, particularly in the chorus where you have some larger intervallic leaps to manage with secure intonation maintained.

The phrases in both verses and chorus will need good breath support applied and with clarity and conviction on the lyrics in order to tell a convincing story with clear diction.

'Key Features to Implement at this Grade' are shown in the *Repertoire Overview* on page 6.

It Means Beautiful

from EVERYBODY'S TALKING ABOUT JAMIE
Words and Music by Daniel Sells and Tom MacRae

Courtney Bowman

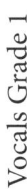

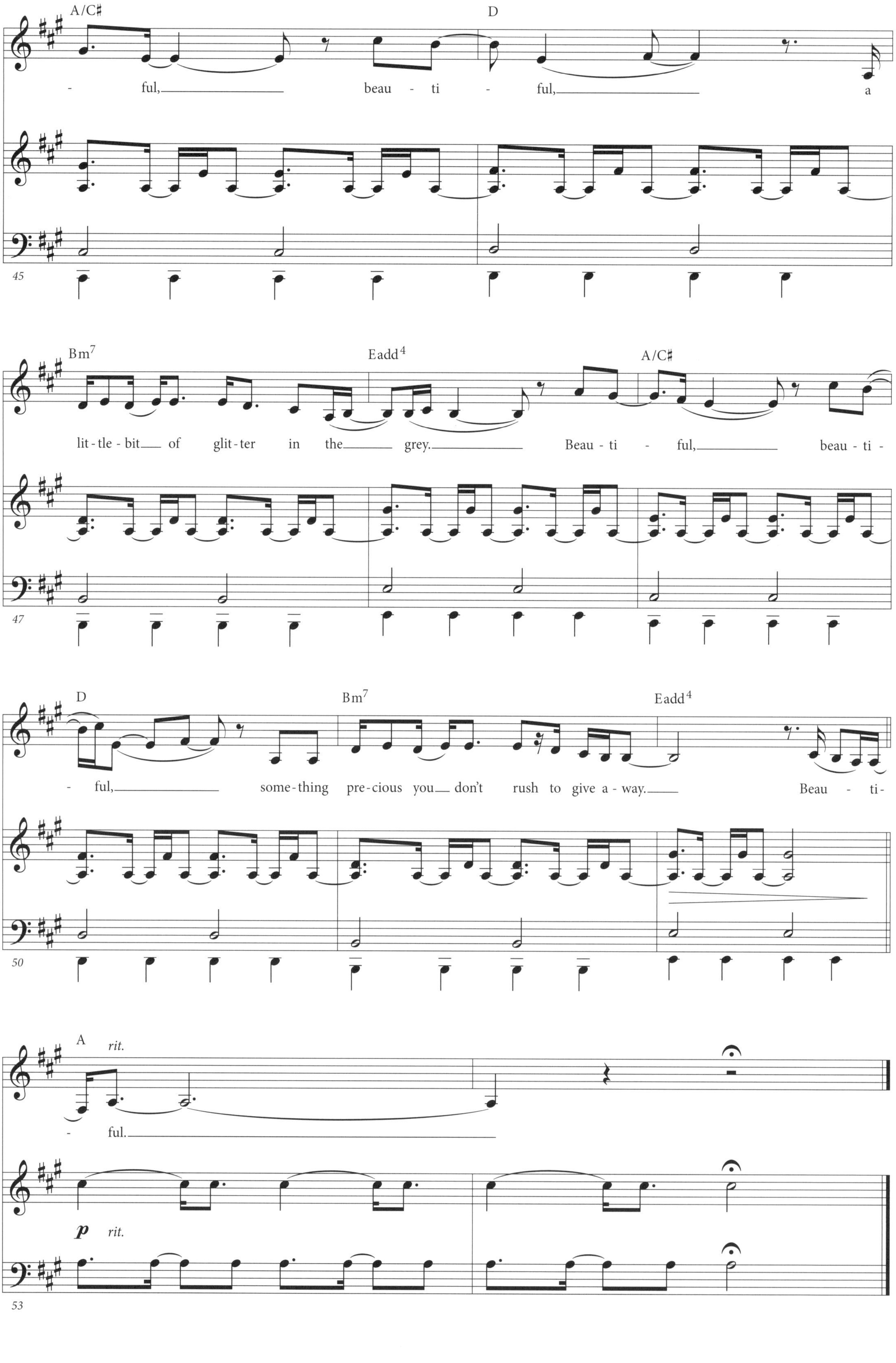

A/C♯
D
- ful, beau - ti - ful, a
45
Bm7
Eadd4
A/C♯
lit-tle-bit of glit-ter in the grey. Beau - ti - ful, beau - ti -
47
D
Bm7
Eadd4
- ful, some-thing pre-cious you don't rush to give a-way. Beau - ti-
50
A
rit.
- ful.
p
rit.
53

Technical Exercises

Group A: Scales

The major scale should be prepared as shown below. The example below is shown from the starting note of A3, however, you may perform it *from a starting note of your choice*. Please note: the examiner can play starting notes in the range A3–G♯4, but you may sing *in any octave*.

This test is performed to a compulsory metronome click. The examiner will ask you which starting note you have chosen. You will hear the starting note followed by a one-bar (four click) count-in. You may perform this test using any vocal sound except humming or whistling. The tempo is ♩=80.

Major scale

Group B: Arpeggios

In this group, *both* of the arpeggio patterns need to be prepared as shown below. You will be asked to perform *one* of them in the exam, as chosen by the examiner. The examples are shown on the starting note of A3, but you may perform them *from a starting note of your choice*. Please note: the examiner can play starting notes in the range A3–G♯4, but you may sing *in any* octave.

This test is performed to a compulsory metronome click. The examiner will ask you which starting note you have chosen. You will hear the starting note followed by a one-bar (four click) count-in. You may perform this test using any vocal sound except humming or whistling. The tempo is ♩=80.

A major arpeggio | Pattern 1

A major arpeggio | Pattern 2

Technical Exercises

Group C: Intervals

In this group, *both* the major 2nd and major 3rd intervals need to be prepared as shown below. You will be asked to perform *one* of them in the exam, as chosen by the examiner. The examples below are shown on the starting note of F4, but you may perform them *from a starting note of your choice*. Please note: the examiner can play starting notes in the range A3–G#4, but you may sing *in any octave*.

This test is performed to a compulsory metronome click. The examiner will ask you which starting note you have chosen. You will hear the starting note followed by a one-bar (four click) count-in. You may perform this test using any vocal sound except humming or whistling. The tempo is ♩=90.

Major 2nd interval

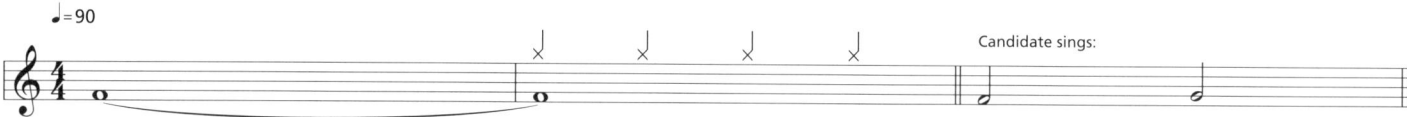

Major 3rd interval

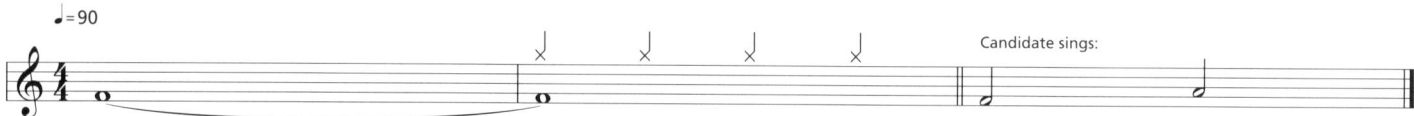

Technical Exercises

Group D: Technical Studies

You must prepare *both* the rhythmic and melodic studies in this group, as shown below. The examiner will ask you to perform *one* of them in the exam. For the melodic study you may choose option 1 (in C major) or option 2 (in F major). If the examiner requests the melodic study, they will also ask which key/option you have chosen.

The rhythmic test starts with a four-beat count. The melodic test starts with a root note followed by a four-beat count. Both tests should be performed to the appropriate backing track which can be found in the audio.

1. Rhythmic | Rhythmic accuracy

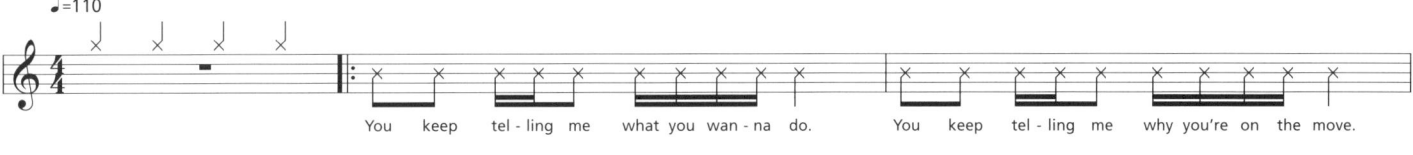
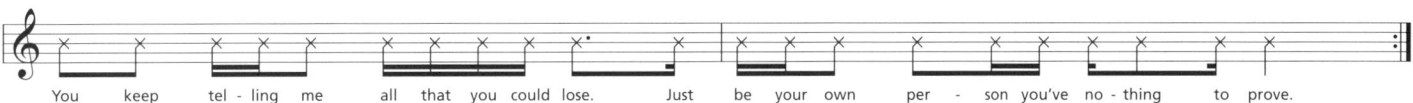

2. Melodic | Dynamic change

Option 1 (C major)

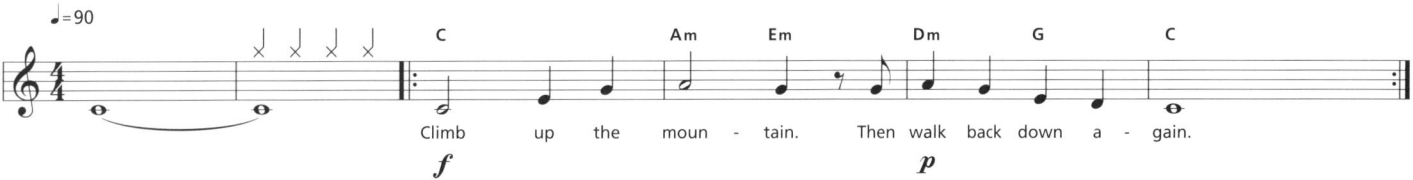

Option 2 (F major)

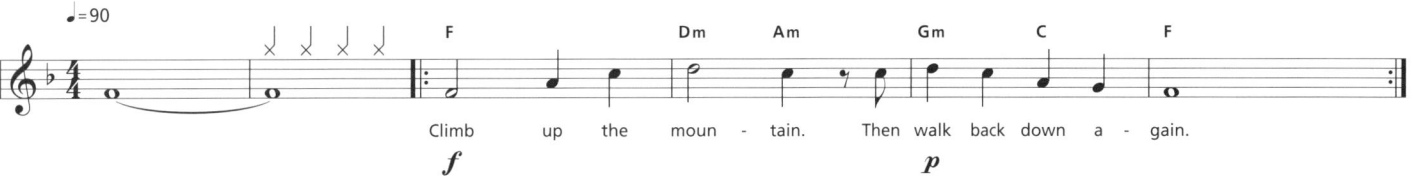

Sight Reading

In this section you have a choice between:

- *Either* – a Sight Reading test
- *Or* – an Improvisation & Interpretation test (see facing page).

The examiner will ask you which one you wish to choose before commencing. Once you have decided, you cannot change your mind.

The examiner will give you a four-bar melody in the key of C major covering a range up to a major 3rd. You will be given 90 seconds to practise, after which you will perform the test. The tempo is ♩=70.

During the practise time you will be given the choice of a metronome click throughout or a count-in of four beats at the beginning. Whichever option you choose, the practise time will start with the examiner playing the root note. You will receive the same choice when performing the test. The test will start with the root note.

You may perform this test using any vocal sound except humming or whistling.

Please note: the test shown is an example. The examiner will give you a different version in the exam.

Improvisation & Interpretation

The examiner will give you a four-bar chord sequence in the key of C major. You must improvise a melody over the backing track. The test will be based on chords I, IV and V and will start and finish on the root chord (C).

You will hear the backing track three times. The first and second time is for you to rehearse and the third time is for you to perform the final version for the exam. Each playthrough will begin with the root note and a four-beat count-in. The backing track is continuous throughout, so once the first playthrough has finished, the root note and count-in of the second and third playthroughs will start immediately. The tempo is ♩=70–80.

You may perform this test using any vocal sound except humming or whistling.

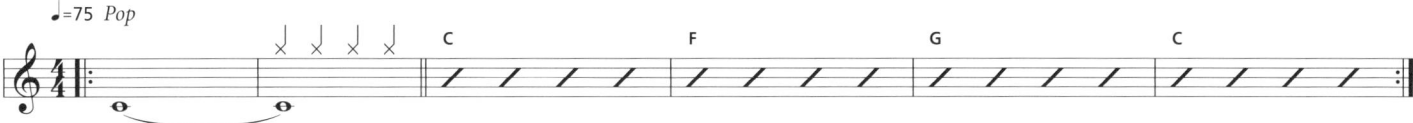

Please note: the test shown is an example. The examiner will give you a different version in the exam.

Ear Tests

In this section, there are two ear tests:
- Melodic Recall
- Rhythmic Recall

You will find one example of each type of test printed below and you will be given both of them in the exam.

Test 1 | Melodic Recall
The examiner will play you three consecutive notes. You will need to identify whether the last two notes are higher or lower in sequence. This means you will need to tell the examiner whether the second note is higher or lower than the first, and whether the third note is higher or lower than the second. You will hear the test twice, each time with a four-beat vocal count-in. The tempo is ♩=85.

Please use the words 'higher', 'lower', 'up' or 'down' in your answer.

Please note: the test shown is an example. The examiner will give you a different version in the exam.

Test 2 | Rhythmic Recall
This test comes in two parts:

Part 1 | Rhythm Recall
The examiner will play you a two-bar rhythm played on a single note to a drum backing. You will hear the test twice. Each time the test is played it is preceded by a four-beat count-in. There will be a short gap for you to practise after each playthrough. Next, you will hear a **vocal** count-in, after which you should sing the rhythm back. The tempo is ♩=90.

For this exercise, use 'da' or 'ba' vocal sounds. You may sing back the test in any octave.

It is acceptable to sing over the track as it is being played as well as practising after the first two playthroughs. The length of time available after the second playthrough is pre-recorded on the audio track, so the vocal count-in may begin while you are still practising.

Part 2 | Identification
You will then be asked to identify the rhythm heard in part 1 from two printed examples shown to you by the examiner.

Please note: the test shown is an example. The examiner will give you a different version in the exam.

General Musicianship Questions

In this part of the exam you will be asked five questions. Four of these will be about general music knowledge and the fifth will be about your voice.

Part 1 | General Music Knowledge
The examiner will ask four music knowledge questions from the categories below. The questions will be based on one of the pieces (including Free Choice Pieces) as performed by you in the exam. You can choose which one. If there are handwritten notes on the piece you have chosen, the examiner may ask you to choose an alternative.

You will be *asked to identify*:
- The treble clef
- The time signature
- Whole-, half-, quarter- and eighth-note values
- A rest in the piece

Part 2 | Your Voice
The examiner will also ask you one question about your voice. Brief demonstrations to assist your answer are acceptable.

You will be asked:
- Where is your diaphragm?
- Where is your larynx?
- What is the difference between head voice and chest voice?
- Why is it important to warm up before singing?

Pre-Examination Checklist

PERFORMANCE PIECES

Piece 1: _____

Piece 2: _____

Piece 3: _____

TECHNICAL EXERCISES

Group A: Scales	Starting note: _____

Group B: Arpeggios	Starting note: _____

Group C: Intervals	Starting note: _____

Group D: Technical Studies	*If examiner requests the melodic study, your choice of key is:*

☐ Option 1 | C major

☐ Option 2 | F major

SUPPORTING TESTS

Sight Reading	*Options:*
or
Improvisation & Interpretation	☐ Sight Reading

☐ Improvisation & Interpretation

Ear Tests	*No options*

General Musicianship Questions	*No options (both sections must be prepared):*

☐ Part 1 | General Music Knowledge

☐ Part 2 | Your Voice

Entering Exams, Exam Procedure & Marking Schemes

Entering Exams

Entering a Rockschool exam is easy. You can enter online at *www.rslawards.com* or by downloading and filling in an exam entry form. The full Rockschool examination terms and conditions as well as exam periods and current fees are available from our website or by calling +44 (0)345 460 4747.

Exam procedure

In the exam you can decide whether to start with the Performance Pieces or the Technical Exercises. These will be followed by the Supporting Tests (Ear Tests and Quick Study Pieces) and General Musicianship Questions.

Use Of Microphone

At Debut and Levels 1 and 2 (Grades 1-5) microphone use is optional, although candidates may use one if they feel it will enhance their performance. At Level 3 (Grades 6–8) microphone use is obligatory for all aspects of the exam.

Marking Schemes

Below are the marking schemes for the two different types of Rockschool exam.

Grade Exams | Grades 1–5

ELEMENT	PASS	MERIT	DISTINCTION
Performance Piece 1	12–14 out of 20	15–17 out of 20	18+ out of 20
Performance Piece 2	12–14 out of 20	15–17 out of 20	18+ out of 20
Performance Piece 3	12–14 out of 20	15–17 out of 20	18+ out of 20
Technical Exercises	9–10 out of 15	11–12 out of 15	13+ out of 15
Either Sight Reading *or* Improvisation & Interpretation	6 out of 10	7–8 out of 10	9+ out of 10
Ear Tests	6 out of 10	7–8 out of 10	9+ out of 10
General Musicianship Questions	3 out of 5	4 out of 5	5 out of 5
TOTAL MARKS	60%+	74%+	90%+

Performance Certificates | Grades 1–8

ELEMENT	PASS	MERIT	DISTINCTION
Performance Piece 1	12–14 out of 20	15–17 out of 20	18+ out of 20
Performance Piece 2	12–14 out of 20	15–17 out of 20	18+ out of 20
Performance Piece 3	12–14 out of 20	15–17 out of 20	18+ out of 20
Performance Piece 4	12–14 out of 20	15–17 out of 20	18+ out of 20
Performance Piece 5	12–14 out of 20	15–17 out of 20	18+ out of 20
TOTAL MARKS	60%+	75%+	90%+

Musical Interpretation & Free Choice Pieces

Musical Interpretation
Musical interpretation is allowed at all grades in both the Grade Exam and Performance Certificate. Rockschool encourages individual musicality, articulation, expression and use of dynamics when performing. This applies anywhere in the exam other than the technical exercises where articulation when specified must be observed. Candidates are reminded that all musical interpretation should be stylistically appropriate. For reference, the downloadable audio accompanying this book contains example performances of the pieces by professional singers demonstrating their interpretation of the scores.

Free Choice Pieces (FCPs)
Free Choice Pieces are accepted in all Vocals grades. An FCP is defined as any piece outside the grade book, and can fall into two categories:

1) **Wider Repertoire:** a full list of suggested pieces can be found on our website *www.rslawards.com*

2) **Own Choice:** Candidates can choose or compose any song in any genre outside of the grade book and wider repertoire. These songs should demonstrate a comparable level of technical and musical demand to the pieces given in the set selections in the grade books which can be referred to as an indication of appropriate level. Candidates should refer to the Free Choice Piece Criteria available on our website when accessing the level of a potential piece: *www.rslawards.com/music/graded-music-exams/free-choice-pieces*

For all grades, candidates can choose the following number of FCPs in the exam:

Graded Examinations and Graded Certificates:
Up to 2 of 3 pieces can be free choice. (At least one piece must be from the grade book.)

Performance Certificates:
Up to 3 of 5 pieces can be free choice. (At least two pieces must be from the grade book.)

Candidates must provide a device containing the downloaded audio for free choice piece backing tracks. This can be any device with a 3.5mm jack output *e.g.* MP3 player, portable CD player, phone or tablet. We recommend that where possible two different sources are brought as a back-up. Audio must be available 'offline' – it cannot be streamed as we cannot guarantee that good internet connectivity will be available in all venues.

Free Choice Pieces must be available in fully notated sheet music and candidates must bring a copy of the sheet music for the examiner to refer to during the examination. If there is any doubt about the appropriateness of the chosen piece, please contact *freechoicepieces@rslawards.com*

For a full list of vocals wider repertoire, and more information on free choice pieces including free choice piece criteria, please visit *www.rslawards.com/free-choice-pieces*

Copyright Information

Don't Stop the Music
(Hermansen/Storm/Eriksen/Jackson)
Sony Music Publishing (UK) Limited/EMI Music Publishing Ltd.

Fireflies
(Young)
Universal/MCA Music Limited

Friends
(Tidebrink/Riemenschneider/Mupani)
Universal Music Publishing Limited/Budde Music UK/Copyright Control

How Far I'll Go
(Miranda)
Universal Music Publishing Limited

I Love You
(O'Connell/O'Connell)
Universal/MCA Music Limited/Kobalt Music Publishing Ltd.

It Means Beautiful
(Sells/MacRae)
Universal Music Publishing Limited/Copyright Control

A Million Dreams
(Pasek/Paul)
Emi Music Publishing Ltd (Twentieth Century Fox)/Kobalt Music Publishing Ltd.

Somewhere Only We Know
(Rice-Oxley/Hughes/Chaplin)
Universal Music Publishing MGB Limited

Stand by Me
(Leiber/Stoller/King)
Sony Music Publishing (UK) Limited

We Will Rock You
(May)
EMI Music Publishing Ltd.

mcps